STICK IT TO 'EM!

with *Maxine*

Sticky Notes
with Attitude

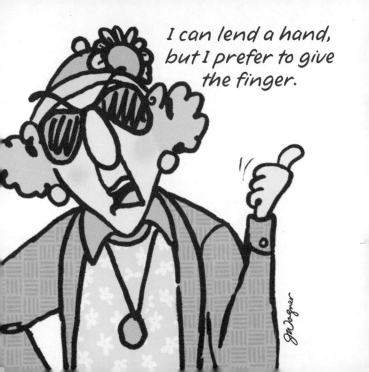

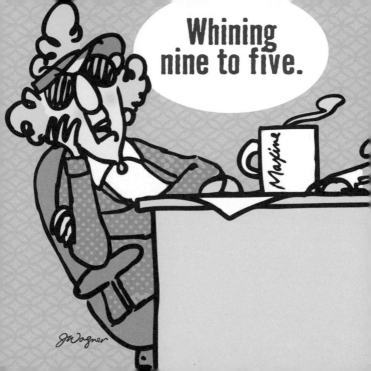

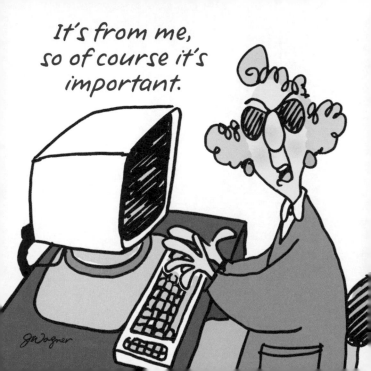

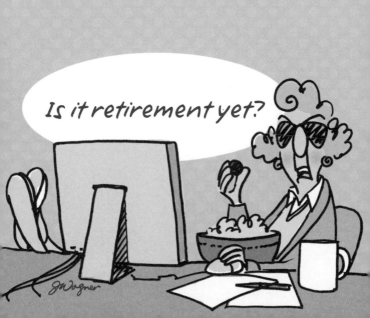

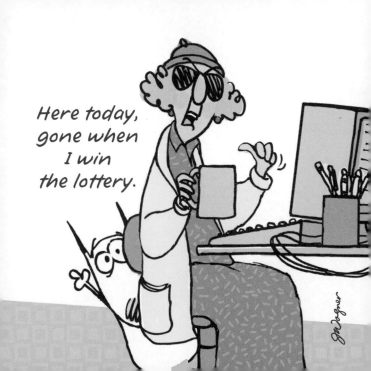

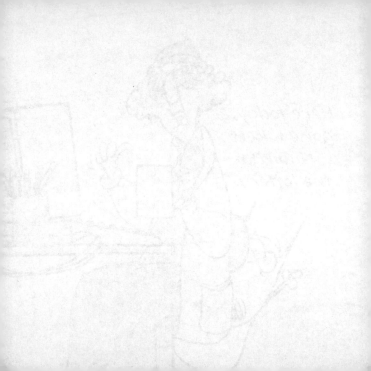

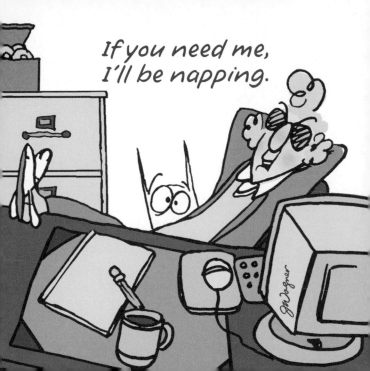

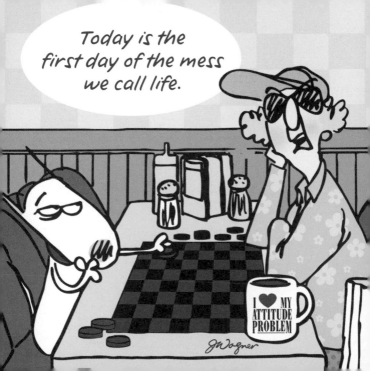

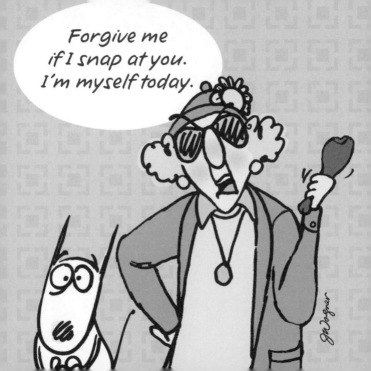

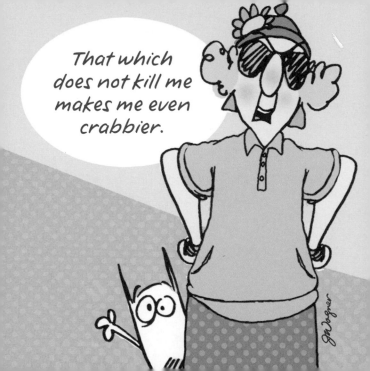

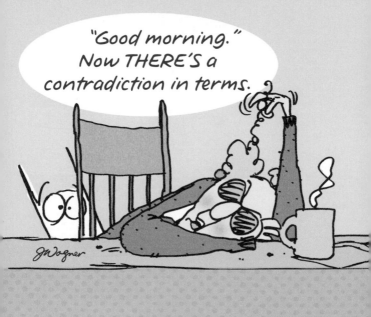

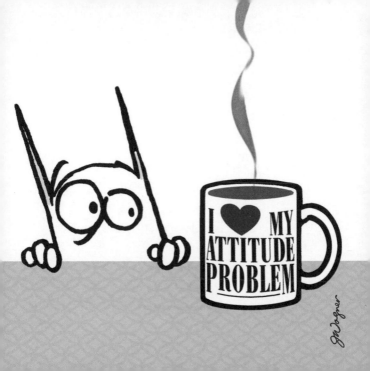

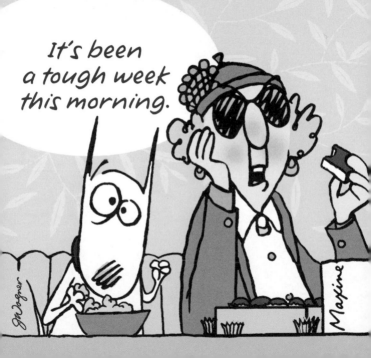

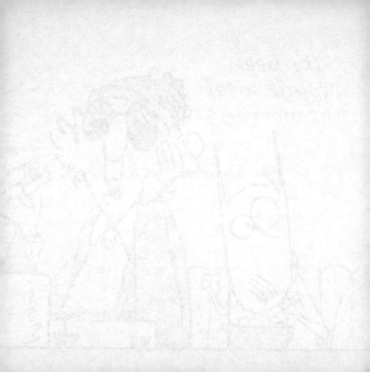

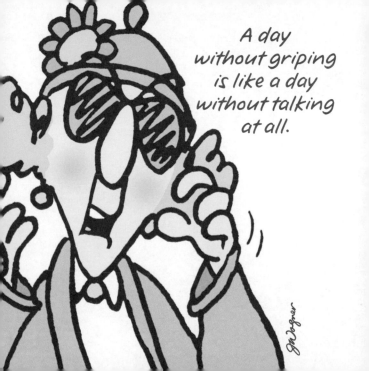

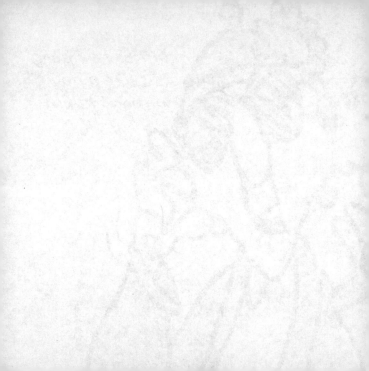

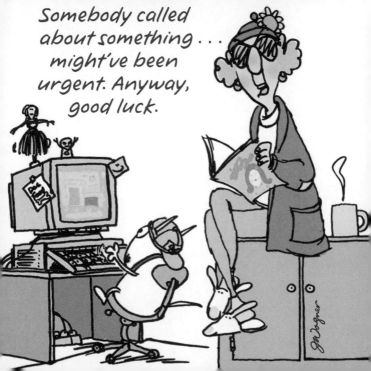

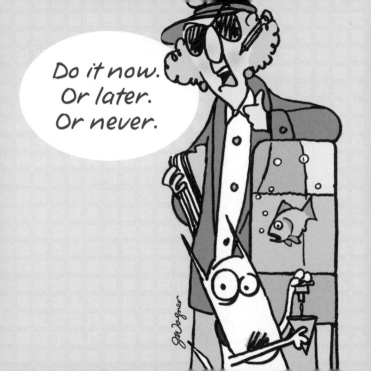

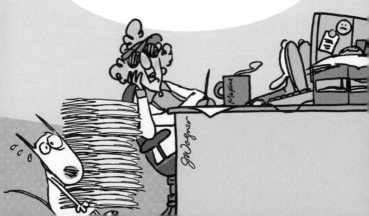

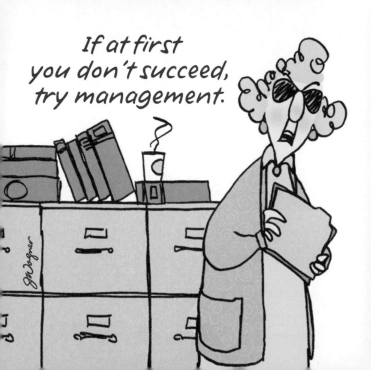

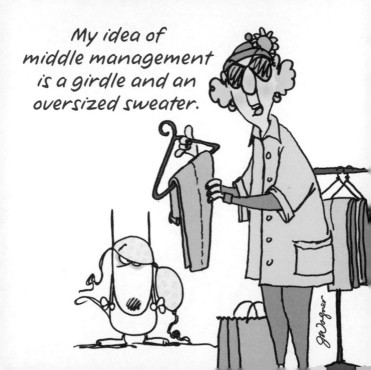

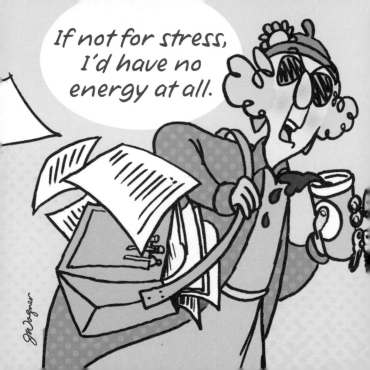

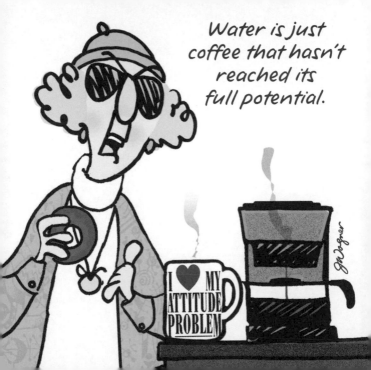

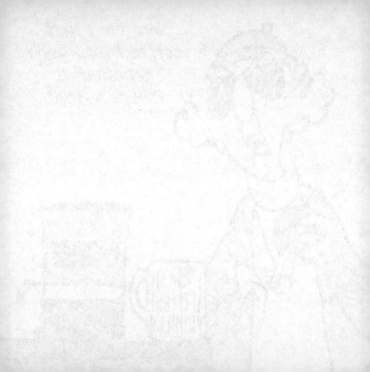

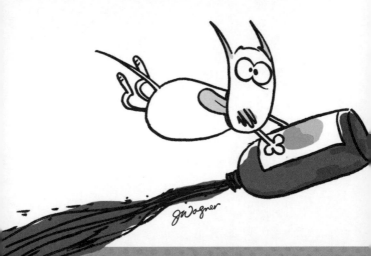

DREAM BIG!

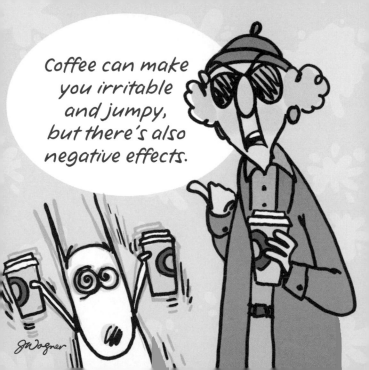

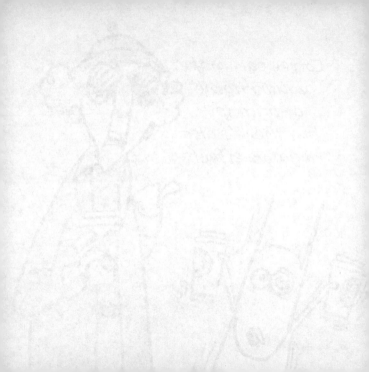

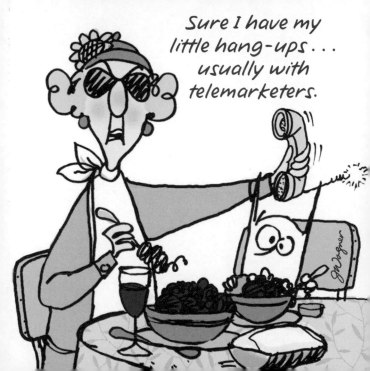

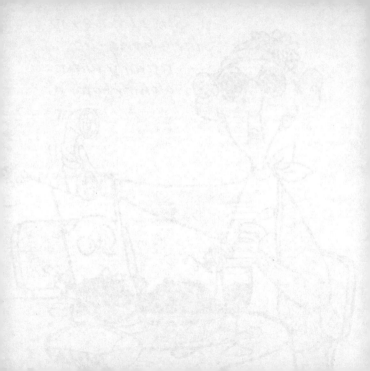

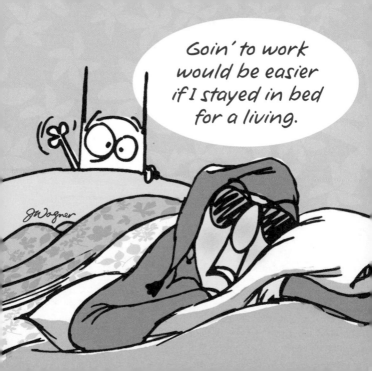

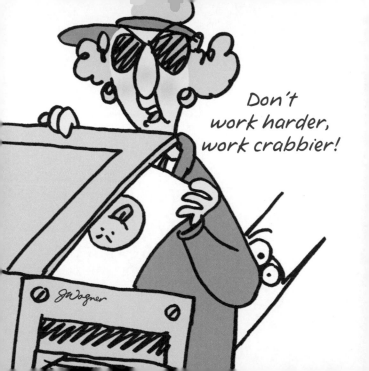

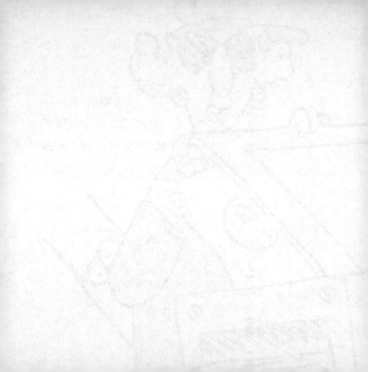

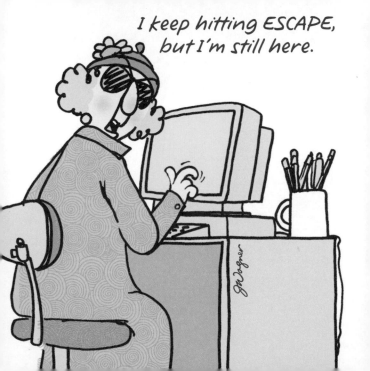

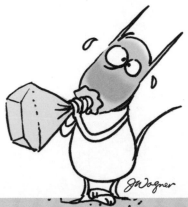

BREATHE

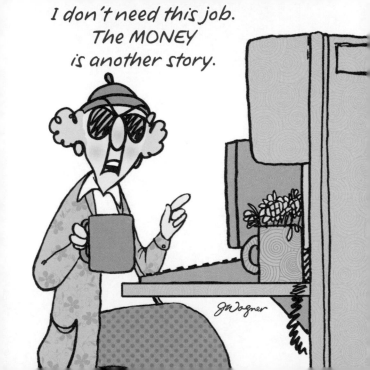

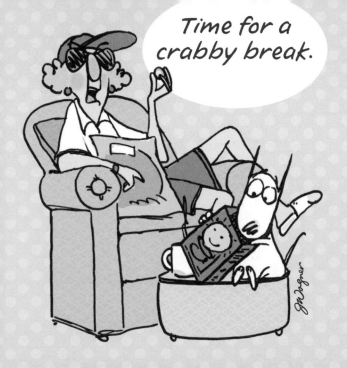

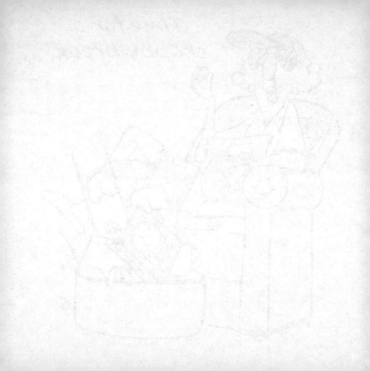

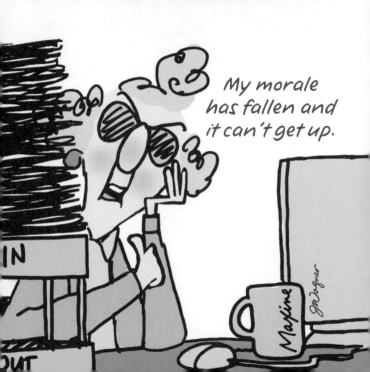

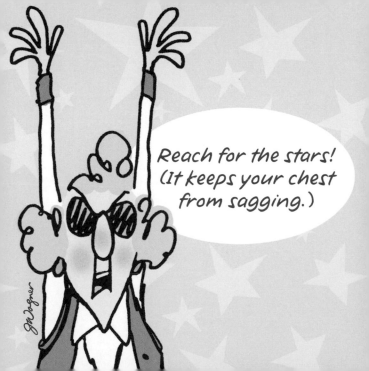

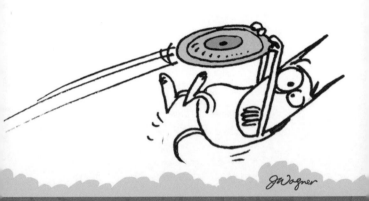

TAKE A BREAK!

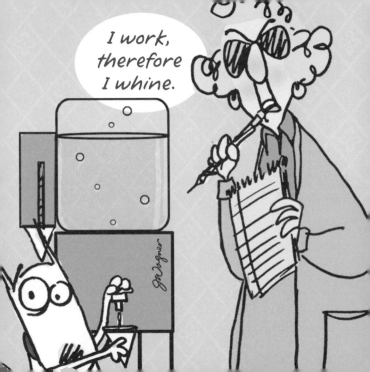

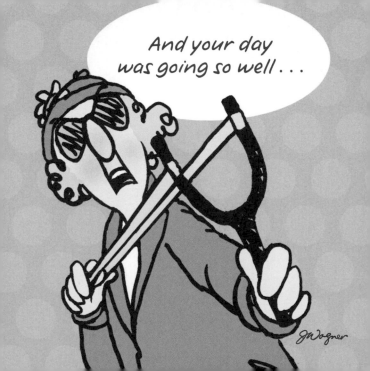

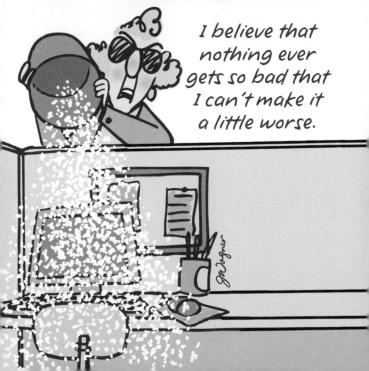

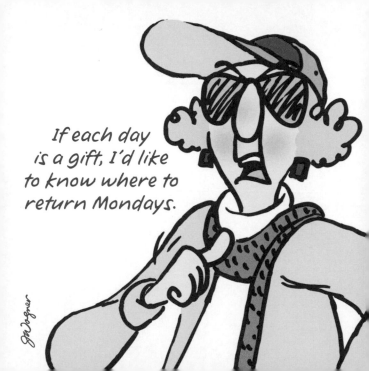

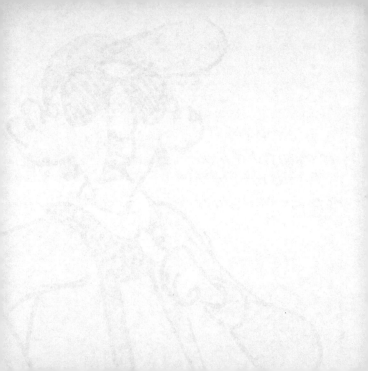

An apple a day
keeps EVERYONE away
if your aim is good enough.

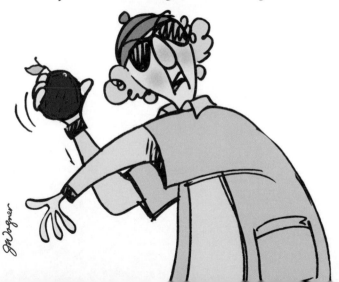

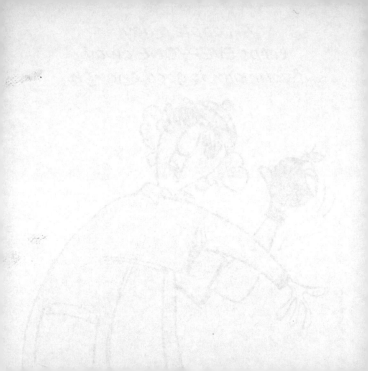

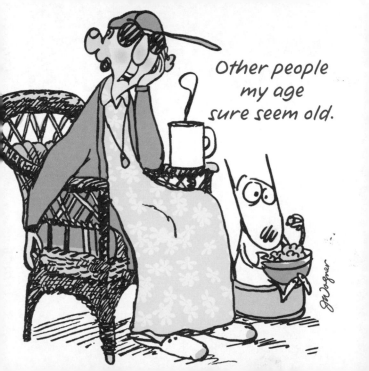

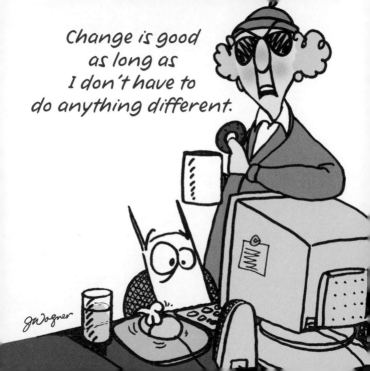

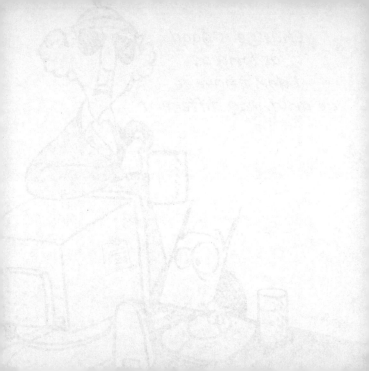

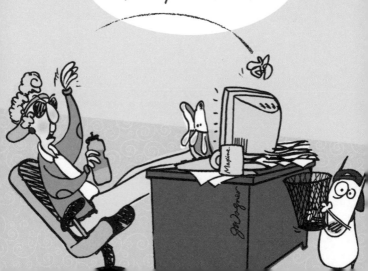

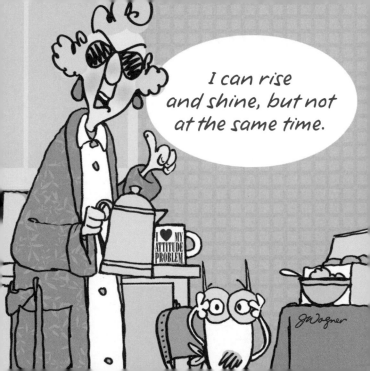

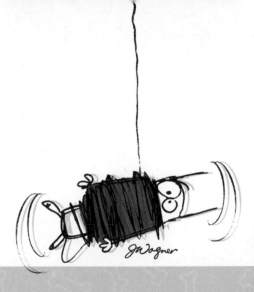

NEED TO UNWIND?

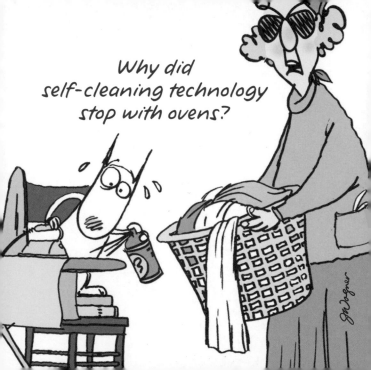

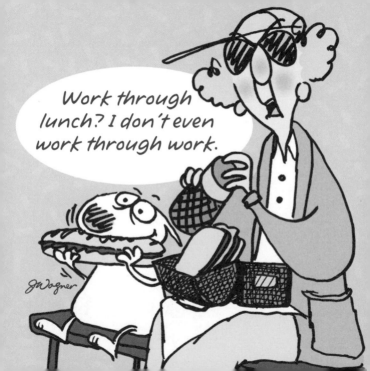

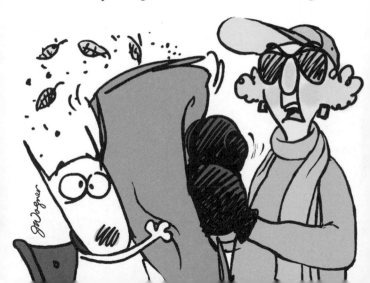

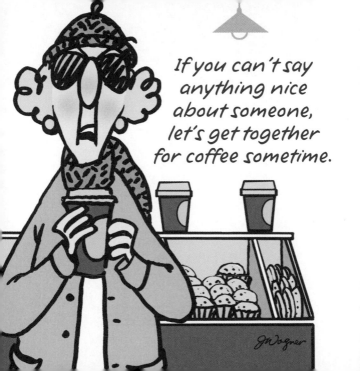

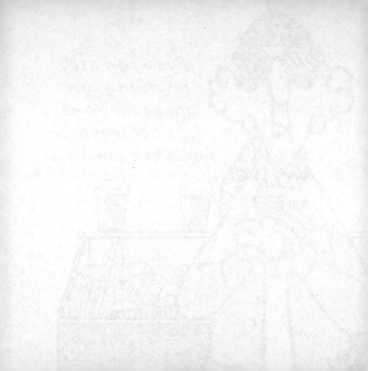

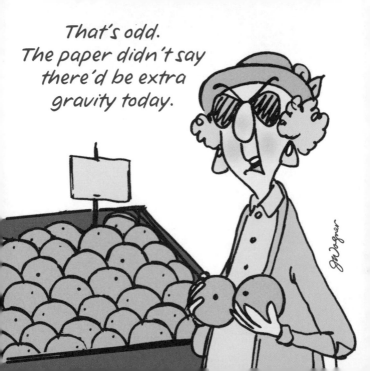

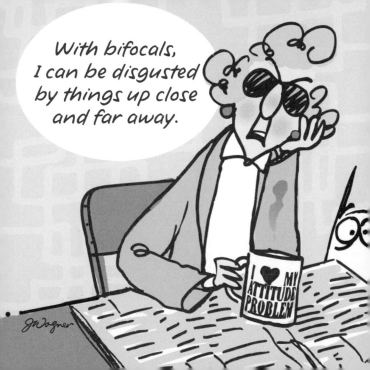

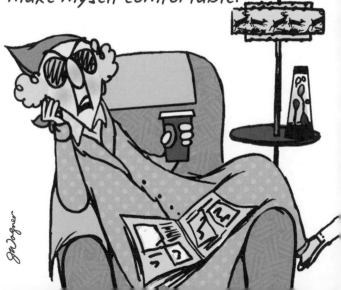

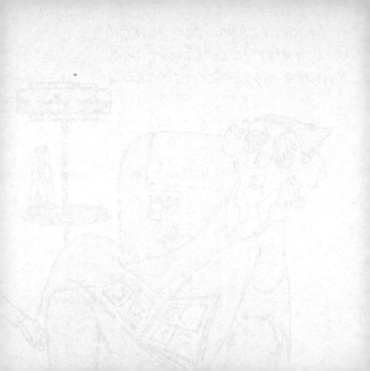

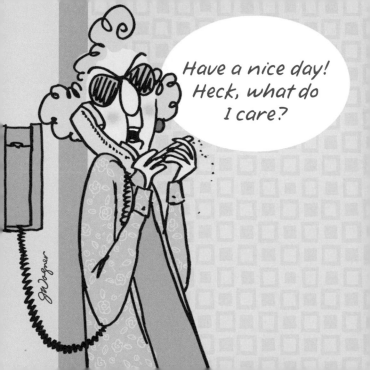

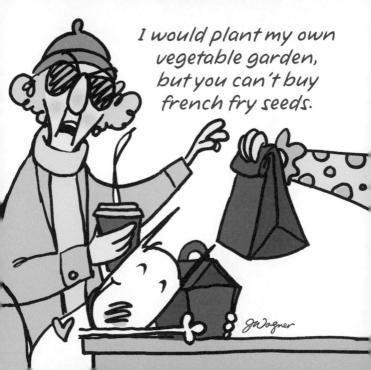

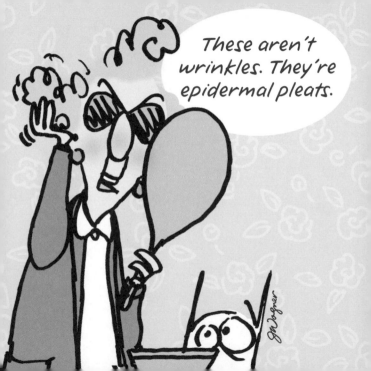

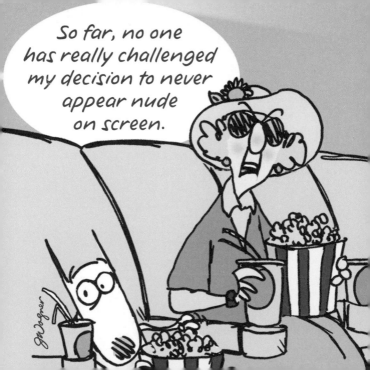

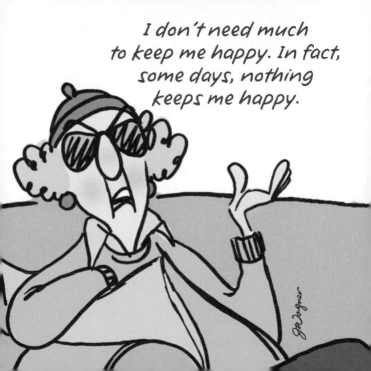

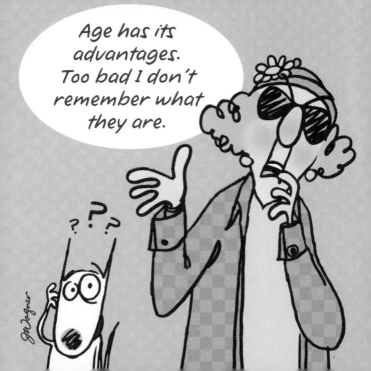

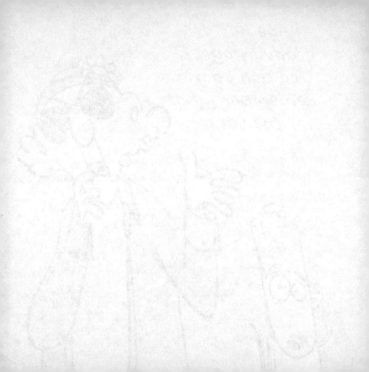

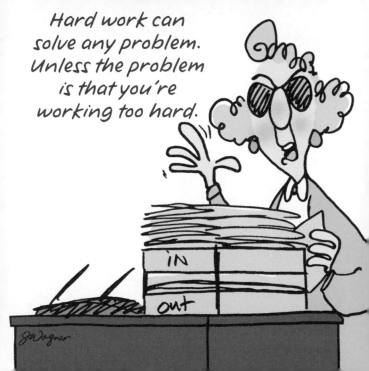

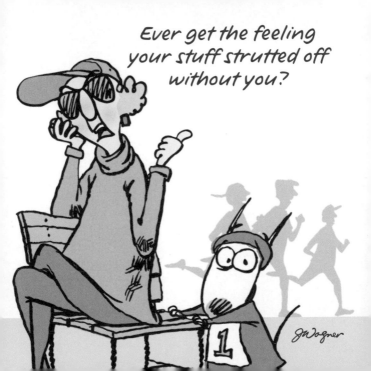

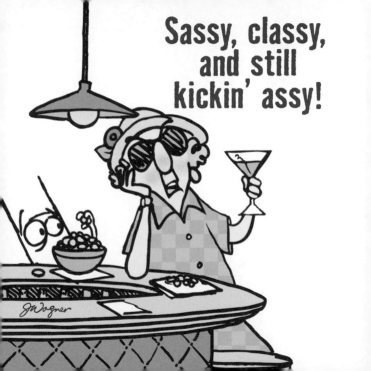

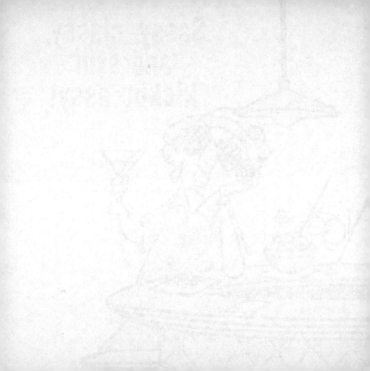

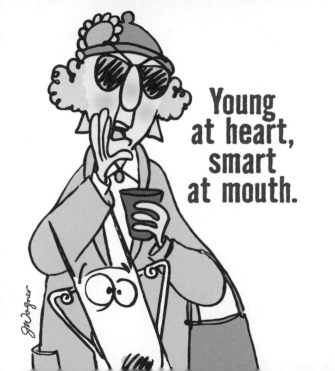

Young
at heart,
smart
at mouth.

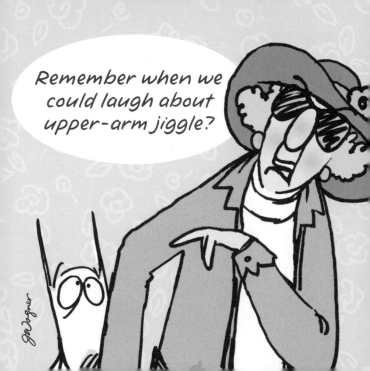

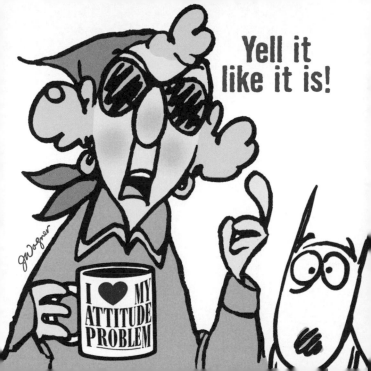

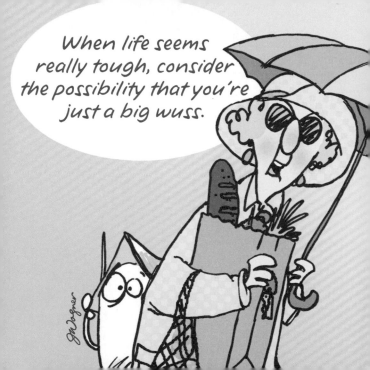

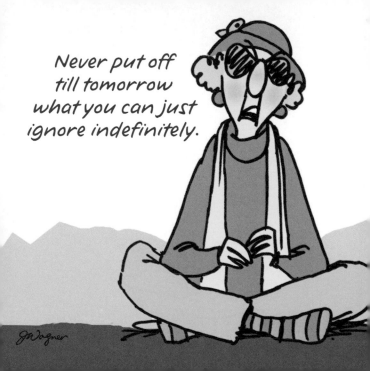

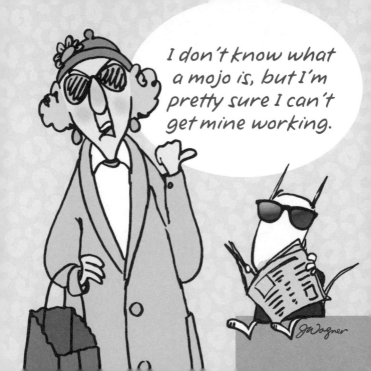

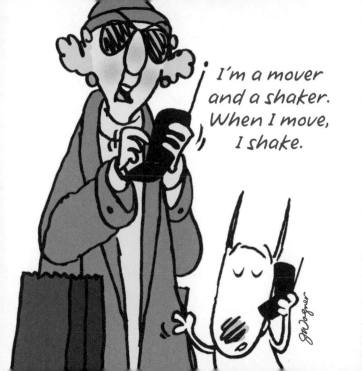

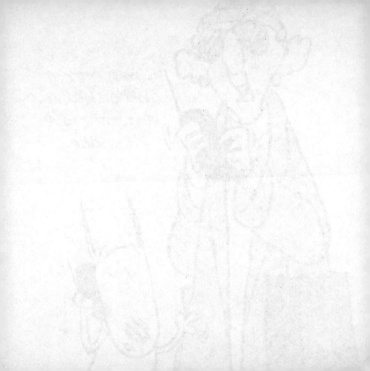

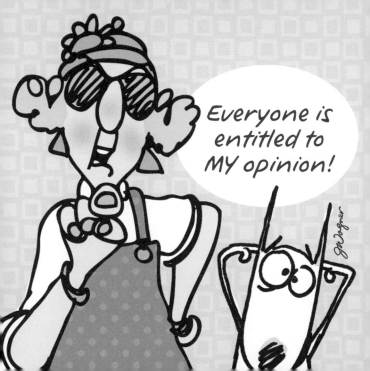

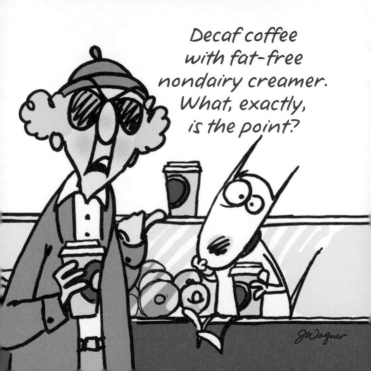

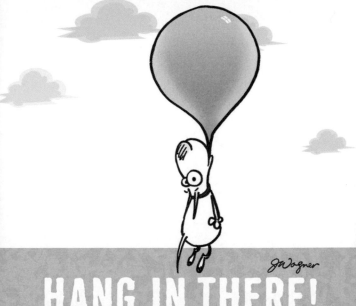

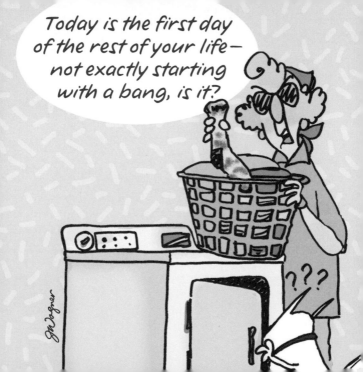

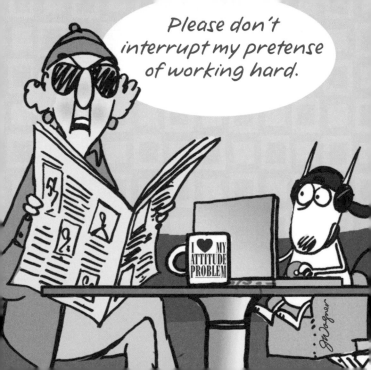

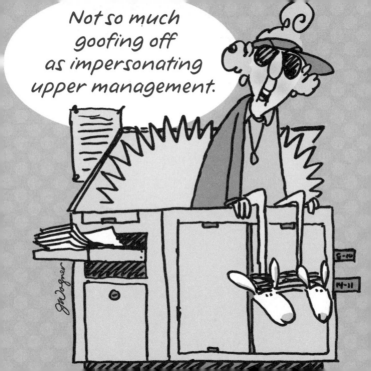

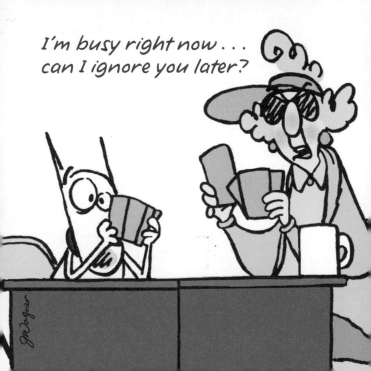

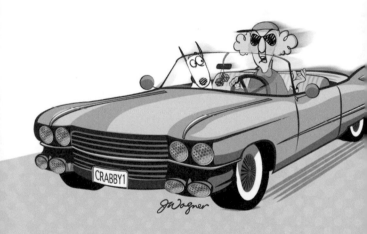

BORN TO BE RILED!

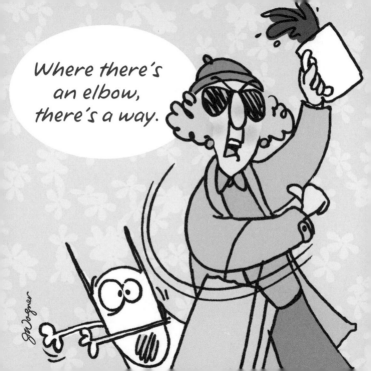

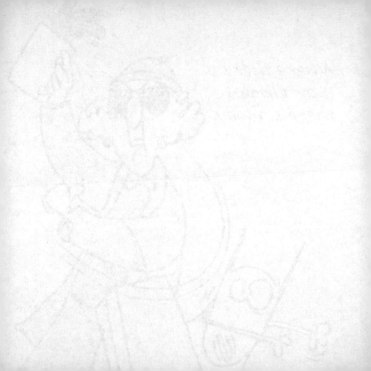

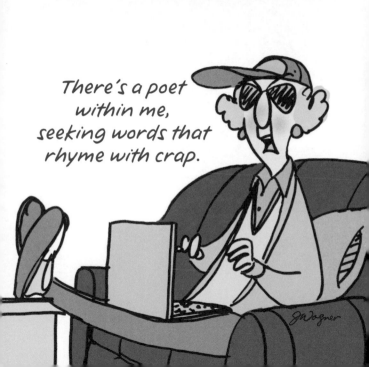

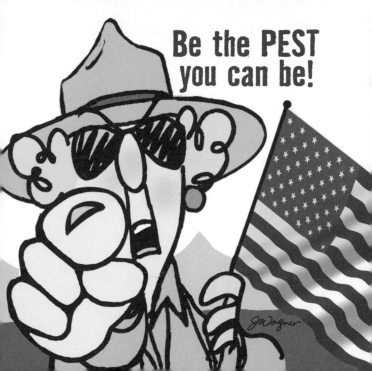

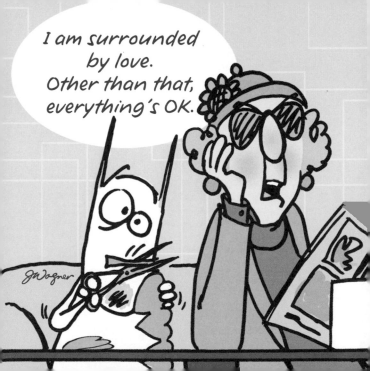

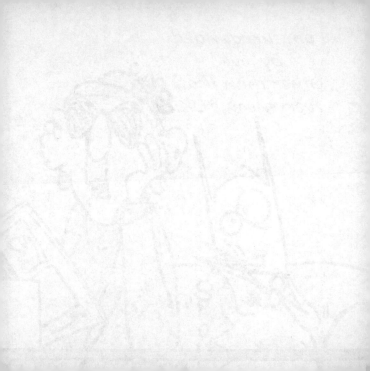

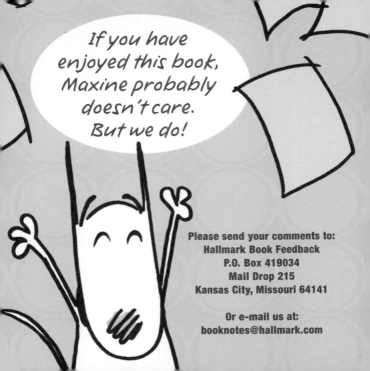

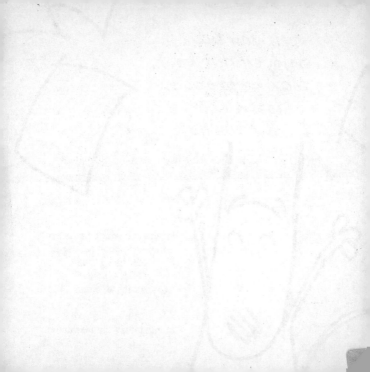